From Feathers to Flames

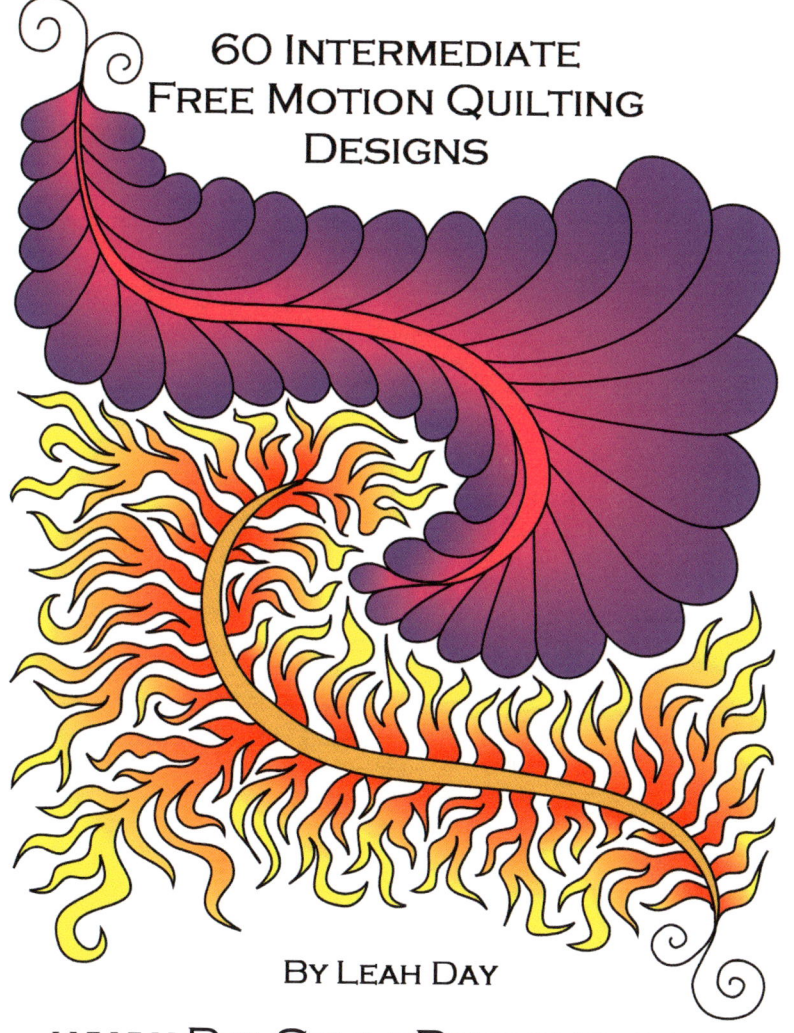

60 Intermediate Free Motion Quilting Designs

By Leah Day

www.DayStyleDesigns.com

Publisher: Leah Day
Graphic Design: Beverly Roberts, Fine Line Artwork, NC
Editors: Josh Day and Chet Day
Published by Day Style Designs, P.O Box 386, Earl, NC 28152

Email: support@daystyledesigns.com

www.daystyledesigns.com

© 2011 Leah C Day

All rights reserved. Apart from any fair dealing for the purpose of private study, research, criticism, or review, no part of this publication may be reproduced, stored in a retrieval system, or transmitted in any form or by any means, electronic, electrical, chemical, mechanical, optical, photocopying, recording or otherwise, without the prior written permission of the copyright owner. Enquiries should be addressed to the publisher.

Attention quilters, artists, and other crafters: Please feel free to use the designs in this book in your quilts, artwork, craft projects, etc. These designs were created to be used and shared to make the world a more beautiful place.

Attention teachers: This book is an excellent resource for teaching free motion quilting. Please go to www.DayStyleDesigns.com for more information about the Day Style Designs teaching program.

We have taken great care to ensure that the information included in this book is accurate and presented in good faith, but no warranty is provided nor results guaranteed. Having no control over the choices of materials or procedures used, neither the author nor Day Style Designs shall have any liability to any person or entity with respect to any loss or damage caused directly or indirectly by the information contained in this book.

Any similarities to existing designs, graphics, or patterns is purely coincidental.

From Feathers to Flames contains 60 continuous line free motion quilting designs originally published on the Free Motion Quilting Project at:

www.FreeMotionQuilting.Blogspot.com

TABLE OF CONTENTS

The Free Motion Quilting Project 6
Filler Design Theory 7
Echoing and Travel Stitching 8
Memorizing Quilting Designs 10
Free Motion Quilting Tips: 11

PART 1 - INDEPENDENT DESIGNS — 12
Stippling 13
Sharp Stippling 14
Circuit Board 15
Hearts & Spirals 16
Tree Roots 17

PART 2 - PIVOTING DESIGNS — 18
Paisley 19
Heart Paisley 20
Butterfly Wings 21
Flaming Paisley 22
Feather Fans 23
Pivoting Designs: Learning Curve **24**
Bleeding Hearts 25
Swirling Petals 26
Pebbled Paisley 27
Pebble Loop 28

PART 3 - ECHOING DESIGNS — 29
Echo Shell 30
Echo Arches 31
Echo Maze 32
Echo Crosses 33
Echo Rainbow 34

Part 4 - Foundational Designs — 36
Topographic Map — 37
Super Circuit Board — 38
Seashells & Waves — 39
Starry Sky — 40
Flame Spiral — 41
Feather Universe — 42

Part 5 - Stacking Designs — 43
Pebbling — 44
Double Pebble — 45
Polka Dot Parade — 46
Fiery Comet — 47
Flaming Cocoon — 48

Part 6 - Branching Designs — 49
McTavishing — 50
Lightning Bolt — 52
Swirling Water — 53
Poseidon's Eye — 54
Heart Flow — 55
Blowing Wind — 56

Part 7 - Edge to Edge Designs — 58
Gentle Flames — 59
Woven Lines — 60
Wiggle Woven Lines — 61
Tree Bark — 62
Pebbles in a Stream — 63
Goldilocks — 64
Landscape Stitch — 65
Feather Filler — 66
Chain of Pearls — 68

Part 8 - Edge to Center Designs 69
Flowing Glass 70
Trailing Tears 71
Icicle Lights 72
Electric Storm 73
Shell Fan 74
Pom Pom Parade 75
Water Plants 76
Cobwebs in the Corners 77

Part 9 - Stem Centered Designs 78
Line Fern 79
Tongue of Flames 80
Swirling Feathers 81
Echo Feathers 82
Butterfly Feathers 83
Heart Vine 84

Part 10 - Center Fill Designs 85
Sunflower 86
Spider Web 87
Paisley Flower 88
Feather Flower 89
Center Fill Designs: Learning Curve **90**
Feathered Hearts 91
Flame Flower 92
Brittle Starfish 93

Motifs vs. Fillers 94

Intermediate Free Motion Quilting Fillers DVD 96
Index and Resources 98

THE FREE MOTION QUILTING PROJECT

In 2009, I challenged myself to create 365 new quilting designs and share them online at: FreeMotionQuilting.blogspot.com

There was only one rule: all of the designs had to be **fillers**.

Filler designs are special continuous line designs that are quilted in free motion without marking or breaking thread.

The designs are created this way so they are easy and fast to quilt using a regular home sewing machine. By not having to mark the designs on your quilt, you save lots of time and will be able to finish your quilts quickly and beautifully.

Each design in this book is created using a simple set of rules that can be easily memorized, **just like memorizing how to sign your name in cursive writing!**

The designs in this book are all intermediate level, but that doesn't mean that they're super difficult or impossible for a beginner to use. Instead, it just means that these designs are a bit more complex and time consuming, but the more you use them, the faster you will get!

I hope you will enjoy the 60 intermediate level designs featured in this book and have fun using many of them in your quilts.

So without further ado… ***Let's go quilt!***

Leah Day

Filler Design Theory

With more than 300 designs published to the project so far, the hardest part is now picking what design to use!

So what determines where a design will work best in your quilts?

It's the way a design is stitched that determines where that design will work best in your quilts.

Early in the Free Motion Quilting Project, I noticed that many designs had common characteristics in the way they were stitched and could be organized into design groups or families.

For example, **Stippling** (pg. 13) is a design that's formed independently of everything around it. The many variations of Stippling all work roughly the same way so they all became known as **Independent Designs** (pg. 12).

There are also many variations of **Paisley** (pg. 19), which all work by pivoting off the starting point of the design, so the whole group became known as **Pivoting Designs** (pg. 18).

Read through the design description at the beginning of each section to learn where that set of designs will work the best.

The wonderful thing about Filler Design Theory is that once you master one design from each chapter, the rest of the designs in that section should come easily to you because they're all stitched in similar ways.

Echoing and Travel Stitching

There are two fundamental techniques to free motion quilting that will be touched on throughout this book.

The first is **Echo quilting**. To echo, you will start with an initial shape (blue arch) and then stitch around it a set distance away.

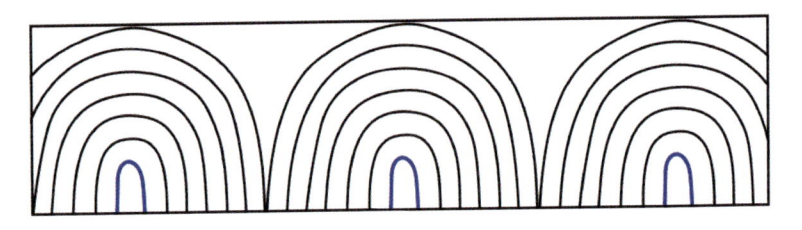

Think of this like the ripples in water after a pebble has been thrown in a lake. Echoes are meant to radiate out of a central object the exact same way.

You can also form an **Internal Echo** of a shape by forming the outer boundaries first (outer flame) then stitching echoes inside:

The key to echoing is maintaining a consistent distance away from your starting line.

The more you echo, the better you will get! Try quilting many **Echoing Designs** (pg. 29) or **Foundational Designs** (pg. 36) for an excellent way to learn this technique.

The second technique you will use quite often while free motion quilting is **Travel Stitching or Traveling**.

Traveling is the process of stitching right on top of your previous stitching. We use traveling to get from one area of a quilting design to another, hence the name traveling!

By stitching right on top of the previous stitching you can avoid breaking thread and keep the design flowing continuously.

Traveling also adds extra depth to any quilting design. Two threads stacked on top of one another will show up darker than a single thread alone, so designs with lots of traveling will always be more dramatic and eye catching than quilting designs without travel stitching.

The key to traveling is staying right on top of the line you're stitching over.

In the drawing on the right you can see correct traveling in Line A.
Avoid stitching off the line as shown in Line B.

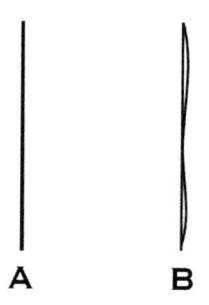

A B

Some designs, like feathers, depend entirely on traveling!

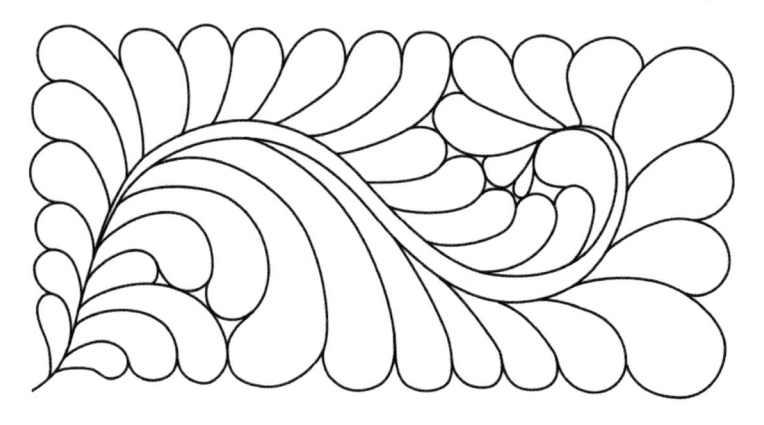

Memorizing Quilting Designs

Are you getting a little worried that you won't be able to remember how to quilt all the designs in this book when you get to your machine?

Don't worry! All free motion quilting designs are created using a simple set of rules, which can be easily memorized.

Think of this memorization just like remembering how to write your name in cursive.

You probably learned how to write words in cursive many years ago, but you've never forgotten the simple rules that govern how the "Q" is shaped or how it connects with the "u."

The exact same principle applies to free motion quilting designs! As you can see from the graph above, Stippling can be broken down into two rules: 1. Stitch a curving, bending line and 2. Never cross this line.

All designs, no matter how advanced or complex, can always be broken down into a simple set of rules.

Once you memorize the basic rules to a design, you will be able to quilt it on any quilt and in any scale, and, just like your handwriting, the better you remember the rules of the stitch, the easier you will be able to fit and fill a quilt with a design!

Free motion Quilting Tips

1. Don't drop your feed dogs - Not all machines are designed to work well with the feed dogs down, and it can greatly improve your stitch quality and tension to leave them up.

2. Turn Your Stitch Length to 0 - Since your feed dogs may still touch the back of your quilt, turn your stitch length to 0 so the teeth will not feed your quilt forward.

3. Invest in the right tools - Here's a list of tools that are absolutely essential for free motion quilting:

- **Supreme Slider** - This is a slick Teflon covered sheet that sits on the surface of your machine and reduces the friction between the back of your quilt and the table top. This makes the quilt much easier to move around - almost like it's gliding on air!

- **Little Genie Magic Bobbin Washers** - These are tiny Teflon washers that go inside your bobbin case and help your bobbin to glide more easily. This results in fewer thread breaks, better stitch quality, and fewer bird nests of thread on the back of your quilt.

- **Machingers Quilting Gloves** - In order to move your quilt easily you need to get a good grip on the quilt top. These nylon gloves have rubberized tips, perfect for gripping the quilt so you have more control over the designs you create.

- **Open Toe Darning Foot** - Darning feet are designed to hover over the surface of your quilt, making it easy to move the quilt around. If you can't find an open toe foot for your machine, consider using a generic plastic foot and breaking it open for better visibility over your stitches.

All of these tools and supplies can be found at:
www.DayStyleDesigns.com

~ Part 1 ~
Independent Designs

One of the most interesting and simple design types is Independent Designs. These are designs based on, or are variations of, **Stippling,** one of the most popular free motion quilting designs.

Independent Designs are all created with a leading line that forms the design independently, filling the space as big or small as you choose.

The key with this design type is to remember the shapes you're stitching, whether it's wiggly lines for **Tree Roots** (pg. 17) or simple shapes like **Hearts and Spirals** (pg. 16), and to stitch them consistently across your quilt.

Texture - Independent Designs tend to have a very flat, directionless texture. While this may not sound very interesting, it's actually an essential component of any quilt.

Any area you stitch with one of these designs will naturally recede and flatten out, making the designs and shapes around it stand out that much better.

Suggestions for Use - Independent Designs can work wonderfully in all areas of your quilts. They can easily bend around complex motifs and look great stitched in any scale.

STIPPLING

Just in case you've never seen the famous free motion Stippling, here she is! I find the easiest way to get into stitching this design is to stitch simple "U" shapes that gradually get more complex:

This can be a tricky design to get the hang of because the rules are so vague: stitch a wiggly line that never crosses itself.

There are some tricks that will make this design easier to master. Try thinking of cartoon letter shapes as you stitch Stippling. Below you can see the letters E, L, H, F, M C, and U which are easy to stitch without crossing your lines of stitching.

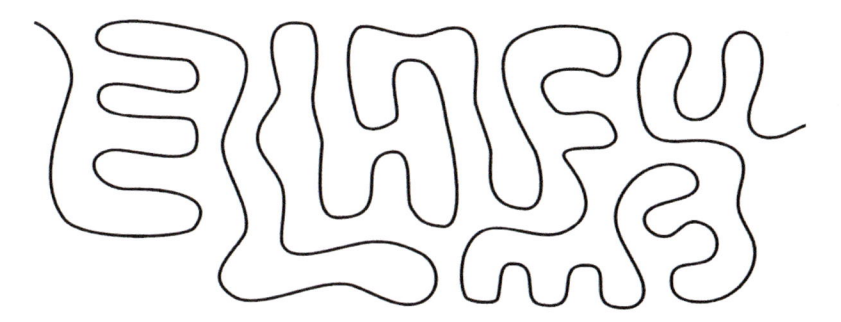

Sharp Stippling

Now let's try a very simple variation of Stippling. Here we've added sharp points to create Sharp Stippling:

To quilt Sharp Stippling, first start with a curving, flowing line. Occasionally come to a sharp point while curving and bending the design around your quilting space. Just like with regular Stippling, try to avoid crossing your quilting lines.

The addition of sharp points creates a very interesting and moving texture. Many quilters who struggle with Stippling find Sharp Stippling easier to master because the points give you a chance to stop and think about what direction to stitch in next.

CIRCUIT BOARD

Points are not the only thing that can change the basic texture of Stippling! What would happen if we stitched the whole design with straight lines and right angles?

To quilt Circuit Board, first start with a straight line. To change direction, stitch two right angles and stitch parallel to the first line, keeping the distance between the lines consistent and even.

It might help to keep certain shapes in mind, like the letters "L," "F," and "E," which can be stitched with straight lines and sharp angles. Having something to think about will help you focus and not get lost in the maze-like texture this design can create.

Page 15

Heart & Spirals

So far we've played with designs where the lines never cross or overlap. This can be really tricky for some quilters, so now let's try a design that requires you to cross your quilting lines.

To quilt this design, start by stitching a simple heart shape, then stitch off and swirl into a spiral. Experiment with forming the spiral shape, then travel stitching right on top of the line to get back out.

Once you form the spiral, immediately stitch another heart. Bend and twist this combination of hearts and spirals around your quilting space, interlocking the shapes together.

TREE ROOTS

Travel stitching and Independent Designs are a match made in heaven! Here's a design that uses loads of traveling to form branching Tree Roots in all directions:

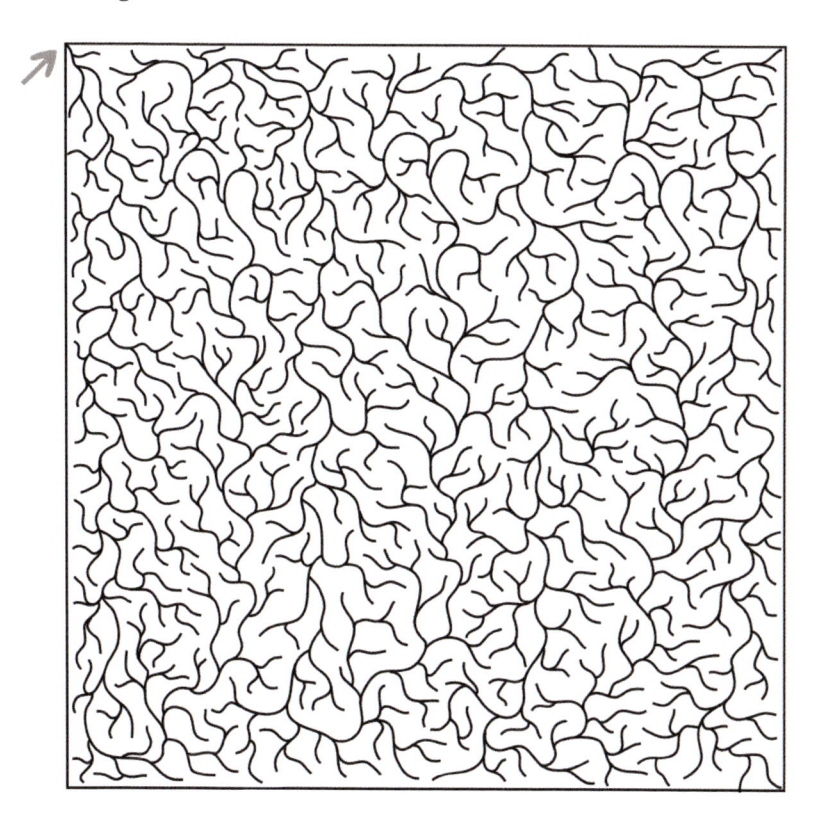

To quilt Tree Roots, start with a gently curving line. Travel stitch back halfway, then branch out with another curving line moving in a different direction. Curve the tree roots around one another to interlock the flowing texture.

The key with this design is travel stitching back down the length of the curving line. This will build up the texture and make the tree roots stand out better on the surface of your quilt.

- Part 2 -
Pivoting Designs

Another well known family of designs is called **Pivoting Designs**. The designs in this family all work very similar to Paisley, and are a fun way to play with many shapes and textures.

Pivoting Designs are formed by stitching a shape, returning to your starting point, and pivoting off that starting point to stitch an echo around your design.

Try tracing the drawing above starting on the red dot. To create a new Paisley cluster, simply travel stitch along the edge of the design and branch out with a new shape in a different direction.

Texture - Pivoting Designs add a beautiful multi-directional movement and dynamic texture to your quilts.

These are the perfect designs to use in areas you want to draw attention to because the flowing stitches and subtle thread play will always stand out from the crowd!

Suggestions for Use - All of the designs in this chapter will work wonderfully in all areas of your quilt. You can easily fit these designs into tiny, complex spaces, or you can expand them to fill a large bed quilt. All of these beautiful designs will look gorgeous when quilted around complex appliqué shapes or quilting motifs (pg. 94).

PAISLEY

All Pivoting Designs are based on this gorgeous tear drop shaped design called **Paisley**:

To stitch Paisley, first start with a single tear drop shape. Return to your starting point and echo the tear drop shape 2-5 times. By returning to this starting point repeatedly, you will build up thread around this area. This gives Paisley a distinctive appearance and adds to its swirling, multidirectional texture.

Travel stitch and branch off with a new tear drop and echoes in a slightly different direction. Play with curving or straightening your initial tear drop shape for a slightly different effect in the finished design.

HEART PAISLEY

One of the easiest variations of Paisley is to change the starting tear drop shape to a heart. You've probably drawn millions of hearts so Heart Paisley should be an easy design to master!

To quilt this design, start with a simple heart shape. You're starting from the bottom tip of the heart and when you return to this point, pivot and echo this shape as many times as you like.

Branch out with a new heart shape, pivot, and echo it as well until your entire quilting space is filled. This is such a cheerful, easily recognizable shape, it's the perfect choice for baby quilts, gift quilts, and of course Valentine's Day quilts!

Butterfly Wings

Sometimes working with a specific shape can be stressful. If you're struggling to form perfect hearts, try these Butterfly Wings based on a free-form wing shape.

To quilt Butterfly Wings, start with a wiggly wing shape. This starting shape is entirely open to your imagination and how you think a butterfly wing should look.

Now pivot and echo this wing shape multiple times. Travel stitch along the last echo and branch off with a new wiggly wing shape and echoes as well. Fill your quilting space with many more organic wing shapes and echoes flowing in all directions.

FLAMING PAISLEY

Now let's play with flames! Like Butterfly Wings, this free-form Flaming Paisley is entirely open for your unique interpretation of what burning flames look like.

To quilt Flaming Paisley, first stitch a wiggly flame shape. The example is stitched with a series of three flame shoots connected together, but feel free to experiment with your own version!

Now simply return to your starting point, pivot and echo that burning flame shape as many times as you like. Occasionally branch out in a new direction with another flame shape and more echoes until your entire quilting space is filled.

FEATHER FANS

What about a feather shape? Can feathers be the base of a Pivoting Design as well? Absolutely!

Start with a cluster of 3-5 feathers squished together. If you have trouble stitching feathers, try stitching a cluster of three or four tear drop shapes instead.

Now pivot and echo your feather cluster, this time bringing your echo line down to connect with the space between each feather.

This echoing style enhances each feather separately and adds more thread play and drama to the design!

PIVOTING DESIGNS
- LEARNING CURVE -

So far, we've learned about a lot of Pivoting Designs that start with a specific shape and are then echoed precisely, so the original shape is enhanced.

A great example of this is Heart Paisley, which is quilted by simply stitching hearts, then echoing with more heart shapes.

Now let's experiment with designs that start with one shape, but are **echoed with different shapes**.

The design below is Bleeding Hearts and it's created by first stitching a tear drop shape, then echoing with heart shapes:

Think about all the shapes you can use to start a Pivoting Design: tear drops, hearts, even free form shapes like butterfly wings, flames, and feathers.

Then think about all the many shapes that can be used to echo the design. Play with combining many different shapes together to create amazing new textures for your quilts!

BLEEDING HEARTS

Let's master this new way of quilting Pivoting Designs with a simple combination of tear drop shapes and hearts:

To quilt this design, start with a simple tear drop shape. Now pivot off the starting point and stitch a heart shape surrounding and echoing that tear drop. Travel stitch and branch out with a new tear drop and echo with a heart shape.

Compare the drawing above to the drawing of Bleeding Hearts on the last page. Do you see how different the design looks when you echo multiple times and build up many more hearts around the tear drop shape? Experiment with echoing 1 time, 3 times, and 5 times to see how this affects the overall design.

SWIRLING PETALS

Now let's try a funky combination! Let's mix some simple curving lines with a petal shape to create Swirling Petals:

To quilt this design, first start with series of three gently curving, pointy lines, always returning to your starting point between each one so they form a cluster of spikes.

Now pivot and echo your spikes with a simple petal shape. Just like in **Feather Fans** (pg. 23), bring your line down between each spike to enhance the appearance of a petal. Play with curving the spiky lines in one direction, then the other to give the impression that the petals are swirling in the wind.

Pebbled Paisley

What happens when we make a row of **Pebbling** (pg. 44) the foundation for a Pivoting Design? You get Pebbled Paisley!

To quilt this design, first start with a chain of 5-7 circle shapes. Travel stitch along the sides of the circles to the beginning, then pivot and echo the circle chain with a tear drop shape.

Pivot and echo around this shape, then branch off with a new chain of circles in a slightly different direction.

This beautiful, slightly formal design will look best quilted on a small scale over the open, uncomplicated areas of your quilts. You'll want to give this design plenty of room to show off!

PEBBLE LOOP

This design looks extremely similar to Pebbled Paisley, but this time the circles fill the second loop of the design, making it easier to stitch on any scale.

To quilt Pebble Loop, start with a tear drop shape, then pivot and echo this shape. Travel into the space between the tear drop and echo and fill this loop with circles, then pivot and echo the entire shape one more time.

Try quilting both Pebbled Paisley and Pebble Loop and see which one is easier for you. It may be easier to quilt the circles in Pebble Loop because you have guide lines on either side of the circles, very similar to **Chain of Pearls** (pg. 68).

- Part 3 -
Echoing Designs

Echoing Designs are created by first stitching a shape, then carefully echoing that shape many times.

Try tracing this design starting in the left corner. Form each starting shape, then travel stitch and echo to expand the design.

So what's the difference between Echoing and Pivoting Designs? The difference is now you must **travel stitch** a distance away from the shape before echoing rather than just pivoting off the starting point. This small change alters the texture and effect of these designs considerably.

Texture - Echoing Designs have a subtle flowing texture and beautiful stitch quality.

Because of the way they're stitched, this set of designs won't stand out and show off as much on the surface of your quilts.

Suggestions for Use - Echoing Designs can easily fit into all areas of your quilt. You control the size of your starting shape and echoes so these designs can easily be expanded to fill loosely quilted bed quilts or shrunk down to fill densely quilted wall hangings. All of the designs in this chapter would look wonderful stitched over pieced or appliquéd quilt blocks.

ECHO SHELL

When I think of Echoing Designs, I usually think of Echo Shell, which is inspired by a traditional Baptist Fan design.

This version is much more free form because you can branch out with shells in all different directions:

To quilt Echo Shell, first stitch a half circle, travel stitch a short distance away, and echo the half circle. Travel stitch again and echo the circle again.

Do this as many times as you like, then branch off with a new half or quarter circle shape, and surround it with echoes as well.

Echo Arches

Just like with Pivoting Designs, all you have to do is change the starting shape to create an entirely different Echoing Design! Here's a fun variation that starts with a simple arch shape:

To quilt this design, first stitch a simple arch shape, coming to a subtle point, then curving back down. Now travel stitch and echo this arch 3-5 times.

Travel stitch along the last echo and branch out with a new arch shape in a slightly different direction. Experiment with the size of your starting arches and the size and number of echoes to see all the different textures you can create with this design.

ECHO MAZE

Remember **Circuit Board** (pg. 15)? What will happen if we combine that design with rows of rigid echoes?

To quilt this design, first stitch a short segment of Circuit Board. If you need a visual image, think of stitching the outline of the letter "E," "F," or "H" in straight lines and sharp angles.

Now travel stitch along the edge of your quilting space and echo this graphic shape 3-5 times. Make sure to keep these echo lines straight and with sharp, 90° angles, so the texture of the design stays very rigid and grid-like, exactly like a real puzzle maze!

Echo Crosses

Straight lines and sharp angles make for very interesting Echoing Designs! Now let's see what happens when we echo a "+" shape to create Echo Crosses:

To quilt this design, first start with a straight line, the travel stitch halfway down and stitch another straight line perpendicular to the first, creating a "+" shape.

Travel stitch along the edge of your quilting space and echo this shape 3-5 times. Play with angling your cross shapes, or even stitch them with a wiggly line for a funky variation of this graphic design!

Echo Rainbow

Now let's play with a much more rigid, regimented Echoing Design. Echo Rainbow is created with many more rings of echoes and is stacked together like bricks.

Start by quilting an arch shape. Travel stitch and echo this line 5-7 times until the shape resembles a rainbow.

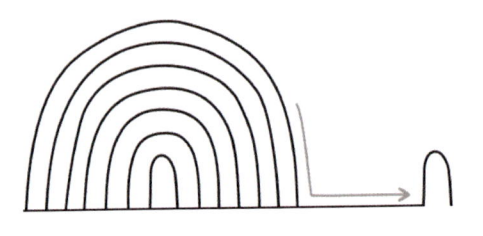

Travel stitch along the edge of your quilting space, estimating the distance so the two rainbows will be almost the same size. The easiest way to do this is stitch across ½ the distance of the first rainbow, so you have the same sized space for the second.

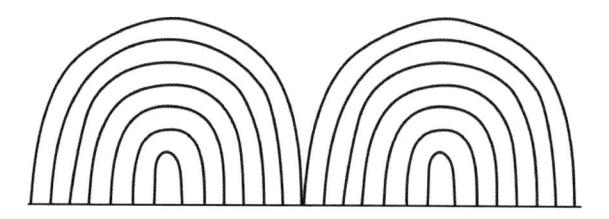

Now stitch another arch, then the same number of echoes, butting the two rainbows together so they perfectly match.

To add the next row, travel stitch into the space between two rainbows and stitch a straight line

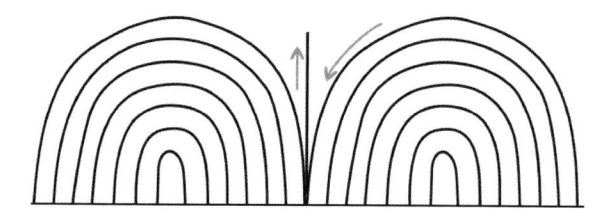

Now simply echo this line until your rainbow is the same size as the ones below. The last echo line should roughly match up with the middle of the two rainbows below:

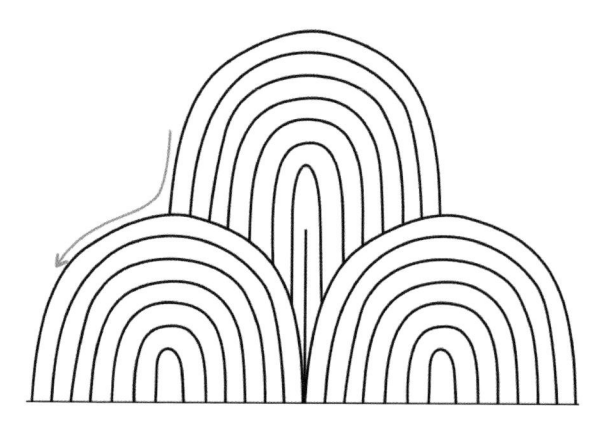

- PART 4 -
FOUNDATIONAL DESIGNS

Foundational Designs start with a single line that fills your entire quilting area and acts as the base for the whole design.

In the diagram above, the foundational line (in blue) starts in the left corner and bisects the quilt space with a gently curving line.

This line acts as an anchor for this group of designs. In the diagram above, the entire quilting space is filled with echoes based on this line. Other Foundational Designs are formed by traveling along the foundation, or interconnecting with it at specific intervals.

Texture - Because the texture of these designs is entirely set by the foundational line, there's an unlimited range of textures these designs could have.

The plus side is Foundation Designs are super fast to stitch because once the first line is set, the rest of the design should be easy to complete.

Suggestions for Use - These designs can easily stretch across the whole surface of a quilt or within a small specific area of a block. Because you need to be able to evenly cover your quilting space with the foundation, this family of designs will work best in the open, uncomplicated areas of your quilt.

Topographic Map

This is a very simple Foundational design which starts with a freeform, gently curving line that occasionally forms bubbles like the lines on a topographic map:

To quilt this design, first stitch a long, gently curving line. Form a round, bubble shape, then stitch off in another direction, keeping this line very open so you have space to fill later.

Once you've filled the entire area with a single, curving bubbly line, travel a short distance and echo this line multiple times until the entire space is filled on one side. Travel to the other side of the foundation line and fill the other side with echoes as well.

SUPER CIRCUIT BOARD

Creating variations of Foundational Designs is easy because all you have to do is change your starting line. Let's try using **Circuit Board** (pg. 15) as the base of another graphic design:

To stitch this design, start by filling your entire quilting space with an open, large scale Circuit Board. Make sure to leave at least 1" between your lines of quilting.

Now travel stitch and echo this foundational line, keeping your lines straight and rigid throughout. Once you fill one side with echoes, travel stitch and echo the opposite side until your entire quilting space is filled with this graphic texture.

Sea Shells & Waves

Now let's try mixing these Foundational Designs up a bit by intentionally connecting with areas of the foundational line.

Start with a curving line and occasionally stitch a loop, like the cursive letter "e." Now echo the curving line, but when you reach the loops, connect with the base of the "e," then pivot and echo around, almost like you're stitching **Paisley** (pg. 19).

This will build up the thread in these areas and create the look of sea shells. It will also subtly change the texture of the design so the shells stand out even better. Continue to echo the curving lines, and pivot and echo the loops until the entire space is filled.

Starry Sky

The addition of small loops in Seashells & Waves created an amazing new texture. Now what will happen if we add stars?

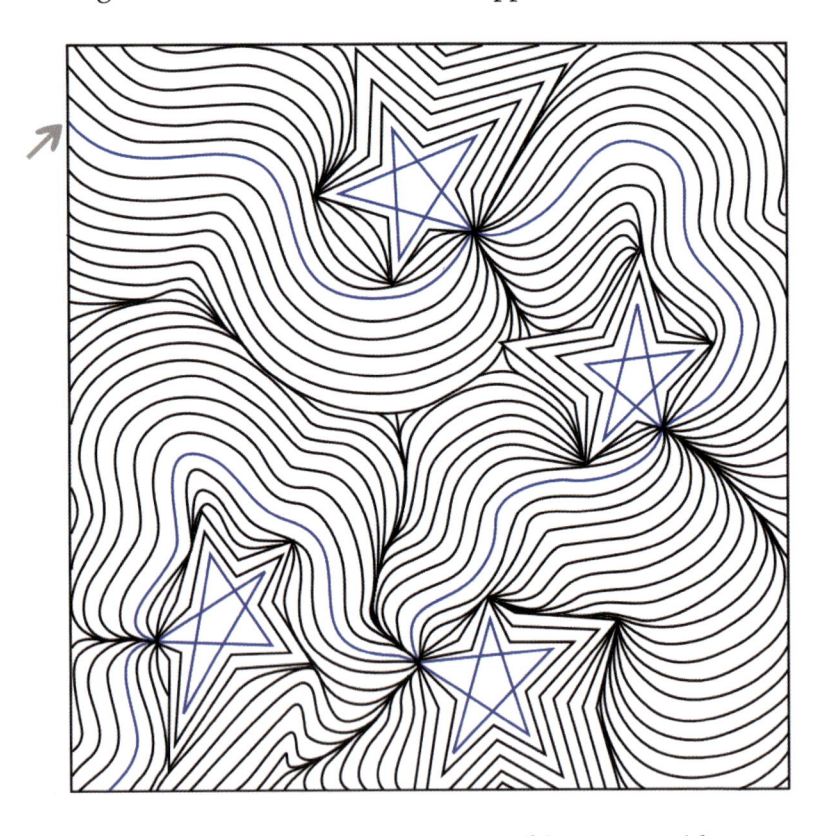

To quilt this design, first fill your entire quilting space with a curving line and occasionally stitch a simple star shape. Now echo the curving line, but when you reach the stars connect with the base, then pivot and echo, keeping your lines straight and angles sharp when echoing the stars.

The combination of straight and curvy lines makes the stars stand out even better! Continue to echo the curving lines, and pivot and echo the stars until the entire space is filled.

Flame Spiral

Foundational Designs don't always have to fill in a random way or with echoes. Here's a design that starts with a foundational spiral, and then the remaining space is filled with flames:

Starting in the center of your quilting space, stitch a large spiral, leaving at least ½" between your lines of quilting. Now travel stitch back inside the spiral along this foundation line and stitch off of it with simple flame shapes.

Play with expanding the flames to touch the opposite spiral line and see how that looks, then try leaving a small gap like you see in the image above. Play with the variations in texture you can achieve when the flames are closer together or farther apart.

FEATHER UNIVERSE

Spirals make for an excellent foundation! Here's another version, only this time it's filled with gorgeous flowing feathers:

To quilt Feather Universe, start on the red dot in the center and stitch a large spiral, leaving at least ½" between the lines of quilting. If you need to, mark this starting spiral on your quilt so it perfectly fills the area you wish to quilt.

Now travel along this spiral line and branch out with simple feather shapes, curving them slightly to one side. Slowly stitch into the center of the spiral by quilting more feathers, building them up and curving them into the spiral so the texture of the curve is enhanced.

- Part 5 -
Stacking Designs

Let's move on to a set of designs created by stacking shapes on top of one another. With Stacking Designs, shapes can be formed in any size or shape, but to move from one design element to the next, some area of the shapes must touch.

In order to move from one shape to the next, you will have to travel stitch, sometimes multiple times over a specific area.

This increased amount of travel stitching can be challenging and time consuming to stitch. Just take your time and try keeping your hands closer to the needle for more control over the area you're quilting.

Texture - Most **Stacking Designs** are flat and directionless like **Independent Designs** (pg. 12), and perfect for quilting in background areas or around complex quilting motifs.

Because of the large amount of traveling, the extra thread play makes the designs stand out beautifully anywhere on your quilt.

Suggestions for Use - You can control the size of each stacked shape, so these designs work well in all areas of your quilts. Stacking Designs generally look best when stitched on a small to medium sized scale, and are wonderfully suited to quilt around complex appliqué shapes or quilting motifs.

Pebbling

The most well know and widely used Stacking Design is called Pebbling, and it's created by stacking circular shapes together.

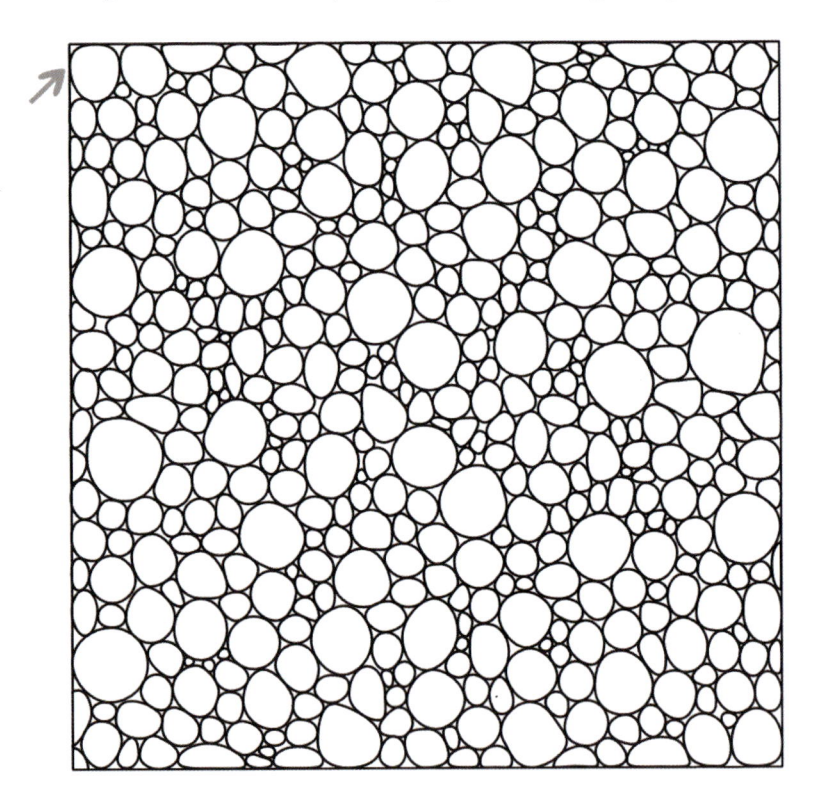

To quilt Pebbling, first start with a circular shape. Now stitch another circle, connecting the sides and stacking the two shapes together seamlessly.

Continue stacking pebbles, filling your quilt one circle at a time. Experiment with this design and see if it's easier for you to stitch clockwise or counterclockwise. Take notes of which direction works best so you'll remember the next time you stitch it.

Double Pebble

Pebbling is a beautiful design, but very time consuming to stitch on a small scale. Try this Double Pebble variation for a design that will cover more space in half the time:

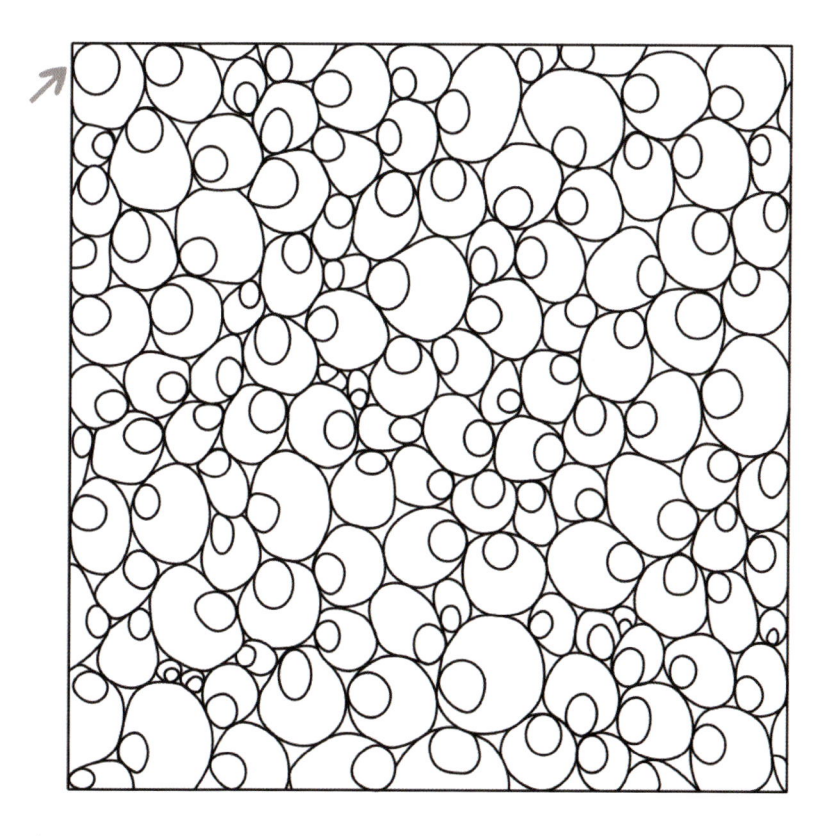

There are two ways to quilt this design. Try both methods and see what works the best for you!

1) Start with a large circular shape, then as you finish this first circle, stitch inside it and create a second smaller circle within.

2) Start with a small circular shape. Keep stitching and form a large circle around this first circle, fully encasing it.

Polka Dot Parade

This variation works just like Pebbling, with one small change: occasionally fill a circle with thread. The randomly filled circles stand out from the rest, kind of like Polka Dots!

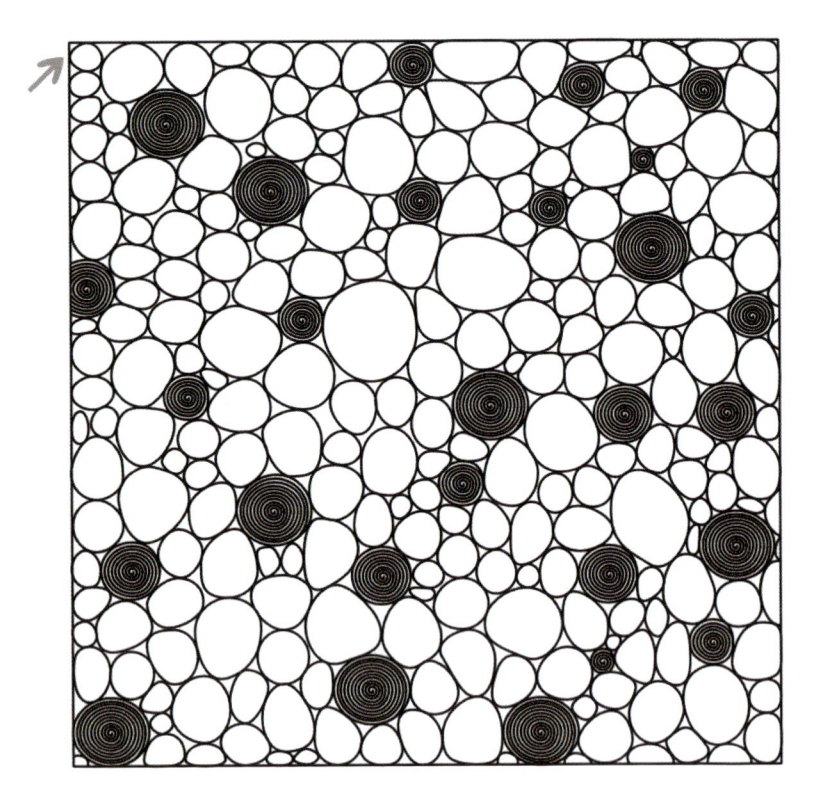

To stitch this design, start with a circular shape. Now stitch another circle, connecting the sides and stacking the two shapes together seamlessly.

As you build the design, occasionally go inside a circle and fill it with thread. The easiest way to fill the circle completely is to stitch a very dense spiral, building up thread until the entire circle is filled and none of the background fabric shows through.

Fiery Comet

Even the most unlikely shapes can be stacked together. Let's see what happens when we stack these Fiery Comets:

Start with a large circle, then surround the circle with a long, flowing flame shape. This will be the comet tail! Travel stitch inside this flame and fill it with **internal echoes** (pg. 8).

Now travel stitch along the outside of the flame and stack another circle onto one side, add a flowing comet tail, then fill the tail with more internal echoes. Continue to stack Fiery Comets together until the entire quilting space is filled with large circles and flowing lines of quilting.

Flaming Cocoon

Let's experiment with the unique Fiery Comet design again, only this time using oval shapes and more echoing lines.

To quilt this design, start with a small oval shape, then stitch inside and fill it with curving arches. Once the oval is filled, surround it with a long flaming tail.

Travel stitch inside and fill the flaming tail with internal echoes until the entire space is filled. Travel to the outside and stack a new oval next to the first and fill it with arching curves, then surround it with a flaming tail. Continue to travel and stack the ovals and flames together seamlessly.

- PART 6 -
BRANCHING DESIGNS

Branching Designs are all inspired by McTavishing (pg. 50) a beautiful flowing design created by Karen McTavish.

All of these designs are formed in the following way: stitch a line, come to a point and echo back to your starting line. Travel along the edge of your starting line, then stitch back to the point. Echo in this manner several times, then branch off in another direction with a new starting line.

As you can see in the above image, by changing the starting line you can dramatically change the texture of these designs. Starting with a wavy line, a zigzag, a spiral, or adding shapes to the end of the line will create new and interesting effects.

Texture - Branching Designs add a gorgeous, multidirectional texture to the surface of your quilts.

While these designs don't have quite as much thread play as **Pivoting Designs** (pg. 18), they will still stand out beautifully on the surface of your quilt.

Suggestions for Use - Designs from this chapter can easily be stitched on any scale, so they will work in all areas of your quilt. Branching Designs can cover large amounts of space very quickly, so they're a great choice for bed and lap quilts.

McTavishing

The mother of all Branching Designs is McTavishing, a gorgeous flowing design created by Karen McTavish.

The swirling lines and light thread play combine to make this one of the most beautiful free motion designs to stitch on your quilts. McTavishing is the perfect design to quilt over water or sky sections in a landscape quilt because this texture could easily indicate flowing water currents or gusty wind.

This texture also looks amazing when stitched over traditionally pieced or appliquéd quilt blocks. If you're struggling to pick the right design for your quilt, McTavishing is always an excellent choice to create a subtle, flowing texture over the surface.

To quilt this design, start with a single flowing line. Come to a point, then echo back to your starting line.

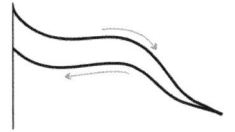

Travel stitch and echo back and forth to the point until you create a branch of flowing lines that resembles cartoon hair.

Travel stitch along the last line and branch out with a new curving line in a slightly different direction. Echo this line 3-4 times, then branch off again until the entire space is filled.

McTavishing has inspired an entire chapter of designs because variations are so easy to create. Here are a few new designs created by changing the starting line to incorporate straight lines, a spiral, a tear drop, and a heart shape. How many more designs can be created just by changing the starting line?

Lightning Bolt

The easiest way to create a new design is to stitch straight lines instead of curves. Here's the first variation of McTavishing stitched with straight lines and sharp angles:

To quilt this design, start with a single zigzag line. Come to a point, then echo back to your starting line, making sure to keep all your lines straight and angles sharp.

Travel stitch and echo back and forth to the point until you create a branch of zigzags that look like a lightning bolt. Travel stitch along the last line and branch out with a new lightning bolt working in a slightly different direction.

SWIRLING WATER

Now let's start to change the formula! Here's a variation that swirls tightly together to create the perfect water design:

Start with a large open spiral, then return to the starting line and echo the outer line. Don't try to go all the way into the center of the spiral, just concentrate on echoing around and building up the outer edge so each Swirling Water cluster is very large and noticeable on the surface of your quilt.

Once you've echoed your first spiral several times, branch out with a new open spiral in a slightly different direction and echo around it many times as well. Continue branching out with new spirals and echoes until the entire quilting space is filled.

POSEIDON'S EYE

Now let's open Swirling Water up a bit and see what happens when we swirl into a spiral, but leave the center circle open:

To quilt Poseidon's Eye, branch out with a long, slightly curvy line, then stitch a circular shape at the end.

Echo back around this circle and along the line back to your starting line. Travel stitch and echo again, swirling around and building up the outer edge of the spiral.

Once you've built up a large spiral around the center circle, branch off with a new curving line with a circle on the end, travel and echo to expand the shape on the surface of your quilt.

Heart Flow

If you can branch out and swirl around a circle, could you do the same thing with another shape, like a heart? Let's try it and see!

To quilt Heart Flow, start with a curving line, then stitch a simple heart shape. Once you form the heart, stop, then echo back along the line you just stitched.

Travel and echo this heart line 3-4 times, then branch out in another direction with a new flowing line and heart shape.

Fill your quilting space completely by repeatedly branching out with more Heart Flow lines and echo quilting.

Blowing Wind

Now let's try another branching variation, this time filling the special shape on the end of the starting line.

To quilt Blowing Wind, first stitch a long, slightly wavy line with a tear drop shape on the end.

Stop at the tip of the tear drop (red dot), stitch inside and fill the space with **internal echoes** (pg. 8).

Return to the starting point of the tear drop (red dot), then echo around the outside of the shape, back to the starting line:

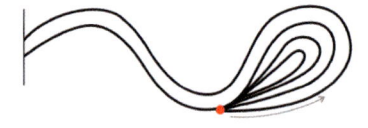

Travel stitch along the edge of the quilting space, then stitch to the red dot and back to the starting line 3-4 times.

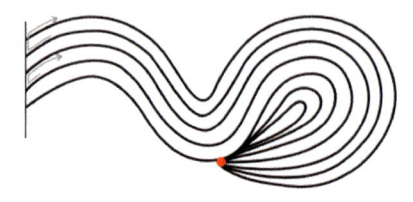

To continue the design, simply travel stitch along the outermost line. Branch out with a new softly curving line in a slightly different direction. Stitch a tear drop shape on the end, fill it with internal echoes, then echo the shape several times.

Swirl your lines of Blowing Wind in all directions to create the perfect windy background for your quilt. This design would also look beautiful stitched over a water inspired quilt to create the effect of flowing ocean waves.

Challenge! Experiment with Branching Designs by stitching different shapes on the end of your initial branching line. So far we've experimented with circles, hearts, and tear drop shapes, but there are many more shapes that could work here.

Then when you're in the mood for more challenge, play with filling the shapes with different textures like **Pebbling** (pg. 44), **Stippling** (pg. 13), or **Paisley** (pg. 19).

With so many textures and shapes to choose from, the possibilities for new Branching Designs really is limitless!

- PART 7 -
EDGE TO EDGE DESIGNS

So far we've learned about a lot of designs that fill your quilt with clusters of shapes. Now let's learn about a set of designs created by stitching across your quilt from one edge to another.

With these designs, you must travel along the edges of your quilting space to move from one design line to another. Trace this design starting on the red dot, traveling along the top or bottom edge to get to each new quilting line.

Texture - Because Edge to Edge designs are typically worked in lines or grids, they usually have a very obvious horizontal or vertical texture. This type of texture looks great when paired with multidirectional designs like **Branching Designs** (pg. 49).

Suggestions for Use - These designs work best when stitched in open, uncomplicated areas of your quilt. Most Edge to Edge Designs are line based and it's very tricky to keep straight lines consistent in tiny areas.

Edge to Edge Designs will work best in quilt sashing because these narrow spaces can easily be filled by stitching back and forth across the space.

Gentle Flames

This first Edge to Edge Design is very simple to stitch, yet it creates a gorgeous, flowing texture that's hard to beat!

To quilt Gentle Flames, first stitch a long flowing line diagonally from one edge of your quilting space to the other, and back again to create a curvy "V" shape. Travel stitch inside this shape and fill it with internal echoes.

Now stitch a new curvy line diagonally across your quilting space to create a new "V" shape pointing in the opposite direction. Travel inside and fill it with echoes as well. Continue stitching across your quilting space with diagonal curvy lines and fill the space they create with internal echoes.

Woven Lines

Sometimes the most simplistic designs can be the most beautiful, and this Woven Lines design is a terrific example of this:

To quilt this design, start by stitching a zigzag line from one edge of your quilting space to another, all along your quilting space.

If you're using this design to fill the sashing of your quilt, go ahead and fill the entire length of the space with evenly spaced "V" shapes.

Now travel stitch inside the first space and echo one side of the "V" back and forth until it's entirely filled with lines moving in that direction.

Travel stitch to the next "V" and echo quilt in the opposite direction.

This is an excellent way to practice stitching straight lines in free motion, which is an important skill to master.

If you find yourself struggling with this design, don't hesitate to mark a few straight lines on your quilt for reference.

Wiggly Woven Lines

Here's a fun variation of Woven Lines that's actually easier to quilt because the curving lines hide many more mistakes!

To quilt Wiggly Woven Lines, start by quilting a long, curving zigzag line from one edge of your quilt to another.

Once your entire quilting space is filled with this baseline, travel stitch within and echo one side of one "V" shape until it is entirely filled.

Travel to the next curving "V" shape and fill it with echoes as well, but this time angling in the opposite direction.

This way the lines are flowing in opposite directions so it appears the lines of quilting are woven together.

Wiggly Woven Lines and Woven Lines both create a gorgeous texture in your quilts

These designs are perfect to quilt in sashing because it's so easy to stitch these designs back and forth across a narrow space. Try them in your next quilt and see for yourself!

Page 61

Tree Bark

Some designs, like this Tree Bark, are more organic than others and allow you the freedom of flowing movement and design.

To quilt Tree Bark, first stitch a long flowing line from one edge to another. Travel stitch and echo this line randomly a few times.

Stitch across again, but this time swirl into a large oval and fill it with internal echoes. Surround this oval with more organic flowing lines to create a tree knot in the texture.

Continue to stitch across the quilting space, occasionally creating swirling knots in the Tree Bark.

Pebbles in a Stream

Let's try another version of that beautiful Tree Bark design, only this time stitching **Pebbling** (pg. 44) in the gaps between those long flowing lines:

To quilt this design, start with a long, gently flowing line. Echo this line 1-3 times across your quilting space.

To form the gap areas, travel stitch along the last line you created, then branch off to create a gap between the lines. Travel stitch inside this area and fill it with Pebbling.

Echo the last line 1-3 times before forming another gap line and filling it with more Pebbling.

Goldilocks

Variations on this theme are endless! Here's another version of Pebbles in a Stream, only this time filled with **Stippling** (pg. 13) to create pockets of flowing texture that look like locks of hair.

To quilt this design, start with a long, gently flowing line. Echo this line 1-3 times across your quilting space.

To form the gap areas, travel stitch along the last line you created, then branch off to create a gap between the lines. Travel stitch inside this area and fill it with Stippling.

Echo the last line 1-3 times before forming another gap line and filling it with more Stippling.

Landscape Stitch

Landscape quilts are some of the most simple and beautiful quilts you can make. Try this design and see how easy it can be to quilt a landscape into the background of your next quilt.

To quilt this design, start with a gently flowing line from one edge of your quilting space to the other. You'll want to make this line quite wavy so you have obvious hills and valleys.

Travel stitch inside one "hill" and fill it with internal echoes. Stitch another hill shape above the starting line, and fill this space with echoes as well. Continue to stack more curving lines on top and fill the spaces between with lines of echo quilting.

Feather Filler

Now it's time to play with feathers! Free motion feathers are beautiful designs that flow gracefully over your quilts.

When learning how to stitch feathers, it's important to see that **everyone stitches them differently**. Give yourself permission to play with these shapes until you find the right angle and direction that works best for you.

Trace the feather drawings above and find the angle that feels the most natural for you to create the smooth flowing shapes.

As you trace, try out these two different ways of forming the feathers off of the central stem:

Feather A - First stitch a feather, then travel stitch along the stem, and form a 2nd feather, connecting it with the first feather on the blue dot. Pivot off this point and travel stitch back along the top of the second feather and branch off with the 3rd feather.

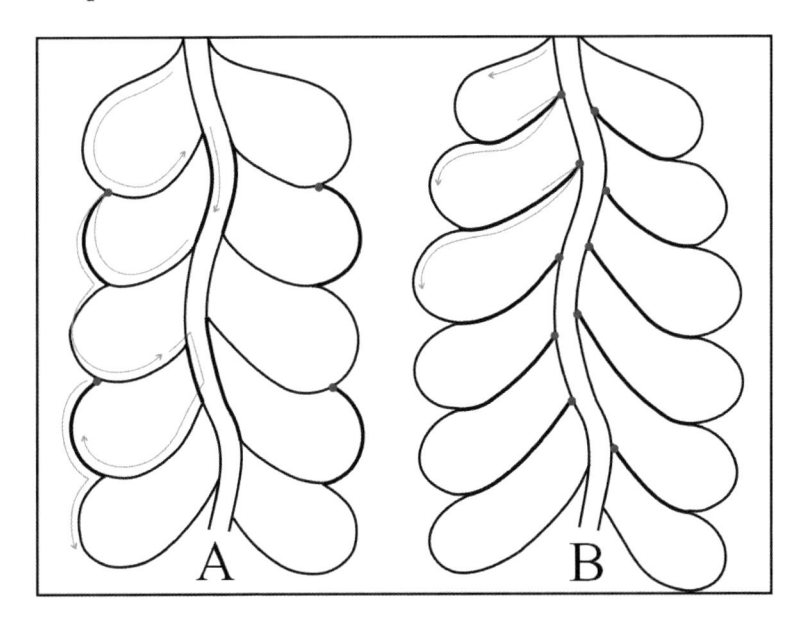

Feather B - First stitch a simple feather shape and stop when you hit the stem. Pivot on the blue dot and travel stitch back along that first feather, then swirl around to the 2nd feather. Again stop when you reach the stem and pivot on the blue dot. Travel back along the edge of the last feather and form the next one in line.

Don't be intimidated by this simple shape! Feathers are just curvy tear drop shapes and nothing to be afraid of.

Feather Filler will fit easiest in borders or sashing because it's intended to be stitched on a straight or gently curving stem. Once you get the hang of this design, try out the more complex **Stem Centered Feathers** starting on page 78.

CHAIN OF PEARLS

Working with feathers often creates narrow stems and channels between the lines of quilting. You can leave these areas open, or you can fill them with a single line of circles like this:

To quilt this design, start with a long, gently flowing line. Travel stitch and echo this line about ½" away. Travel inside this space and swirl around to form a circle that exactly fills the space between the two lines.

Stitch another circle, stacking it right next to the first. Play with quilting circles that gradually change size from larger to smaller or smaller to larger depending on the space between the lines so they perfectly fit in any space.

- PART 8 -
EDGE TO CENTER DESIGNS

Now let's learn about another set of designs that are formed along the edges of your quilting space, only this time stitching into the center to create some really interesting textures!

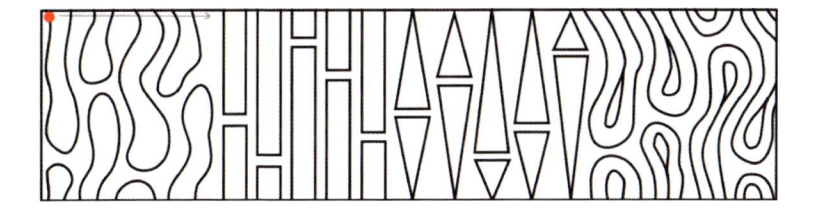

Like **Edge to Edge Designs** (pg. 58), these designs use the edges of your quilt to travel stitch along and fill into the center.

Try tracing this design starting on the red dot traveling along the top edge to create each new shape. To get to the other side of the design, travel along the right side.

Texture - This family of designs might all work the same way, but that doesn't mean they'll look related! Some designs have soft, flowing lines while others are created with straight lines and sharp angles. All of them will create a simple horizontal or vertical texture on the surface of your quilt and look great when combined with other multidirectional designs.

Suggestions for Use - These designs can be tricky to fit into tight or complex areas, so they work best in simple, open areas. Sashing, borders, and open blocks are all great places to quilt Edge to Center Designs.

Sashing is an especially good choice because it's so easy to fill those narrow, open spaces with this type of design.

Flowing Glass

This is one of the first Edge to Center Designs created at the beginning of the Free Motion Quilting Project. Flowing lines of molten glass was the inspiration for this beautiful design:

To quilt Flowing Glass, start on the red dot and stitch a curvy line into the center of your quilt.

End this line with a rounded tear drop shape, then echo this shape back to the starting line.

Travel stitch along the edge and create another curvy globe shape. Play with varying the length of each shape so they are not all the same length.

Fill the first side of your quilting space with this texture, then travel to the opposite side and stitch more Flowing Glass globes into the center.

Interlock the two sides so the curvy globe shapes nestle and interlock together.

Flowing Glass is an excellent choice for the sashing of any quilt. The soft, slightly curving lines will add texture without distracting from your beautiful quilt blocks.

Trailing Tears

Now let's try this easy variation of Flowing Glass by quilting an internal echo within each shape to create a new design:

To quilt this design, start with a long Flowing Glass shape, this time making it much larger with at least ¼" between the lines of quilting.

Travel inside and quilt an internal echo, curving around to create a tear drop shape within the Flowing Glass globe shape.

Travel along the edge and stitch a new trailing tear shape into the center.

Stitch this way all along the edge, filling your quilting space with Trailing Tears of various lengths stitched into the center.

Travel stitch to the opposite side and quilt more Trailing Tear shapes, interlocking them together with the first set.

Because this is a larger version of Flowing Glass, it will fill your quilts faster. This is a great choice for the sashing or borders of a bed quilt you're wanting to finish quickly.

Icicle Lights

Here's a simple design that will add the perfect touch of texture to your winter themed quilts:

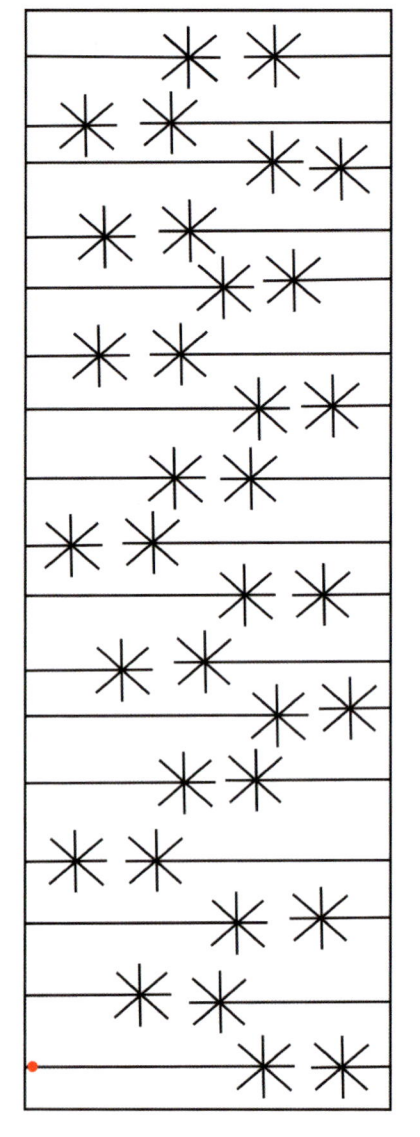

To quilt Icicle Lights, first stitch a straight line into the center of your quilting space.

At the end of the line stitch a "+" shape, then an "x" shape on top to create a simple star.

Travel stitch back along the straight line and along the edge of your quilting space, then branch out with another straight line and star to form a row of icicle lights.

Make sure to vary the length of your straight lines so that some icicle lights are short and some are long.

Fill one side of the quilt with lights, then travel to the other side and stitch a new row of icicle lights into the center, matching the simple star shapes together.

The variations of this design are endless! Play with making the straight lines curvy for an easier version of this design.

Electric Storm

Straight lines and sharp angles make for beautiful designs! Here's a neat Edge to Center Design with jagged lighting bolts:

Start by stitching a jagged line into the center of your quilt.

Come to a point, then echo this line back to the edge of your quilting space.

Travel along the edge and branch out with another jagged line. Vary the length of the jagged lines so some reach beyond the center of your quilting space.

Travel stitch or break thread to move to the opposite side and stitch a new set of jagged, lighting bolt shapes.

When quilting the opposite side, carefully stitch the jagged lines in between the first set so they interlock together perfectly like puzzle pieces.

Select certain jagged lines to connect in the middle and stitch a small star where the points from both sides touch.

The extra stars will add a touch of electricity to your quilts!

Shell Fan

Let's stitch it up a notch and fill from Edge to Center with some simple feathers!

To quilt Shell Fan, start by stitching a long tear drop shape from edge to center.

Travel stitch along the left side of this feather and branch out with a slightly smaller feather. Stitch more feathers, each smaller than the last, until you reach the edge of your quilting space.

Fill the space to the right of the tear drop with more feathers to create your first half circle shaped Shell Fan.

Travel along the edge and stitch a new Shell Fan into the center. Fill one side of your quilting space with Shell Fans evenly spaced along one edge.

Travel stitch to the opposite side and stitch a new tear drop shape, fitting it into the space between two Shell Fans on the first side. Build feathers around this tear drop so the Shell Fans on both sides perfectly interlock together.

Pom Pom Parade

Here's an easier variation of Shell Fan created with overlapping triangle shapes that kind of look like cheerleading pom poms:

To quilt this design, stitch a long, skinny triangle shape into the middle of your quilting space.

Overlap this triangle with more triangles to create a half circle shape on the edge of your quilting space.

Travel along the edge and stitch another pom pom into the center.

Once you fill the first side, travel to the opposite side and fit more overlapping triangles in between the pom poms from the first side.

Try to interlock the shapes from both sides together so they both create beautiful half circle shapes on opposite sides of the quilting space.

If this works with simple triangle and feather shapes, what other shapes will work well in this design layout?

WATER PLANTS

Let's play with a couple more designs that work like Shell Fan. Here's a fun variation that's perfect for a water themed quilt:

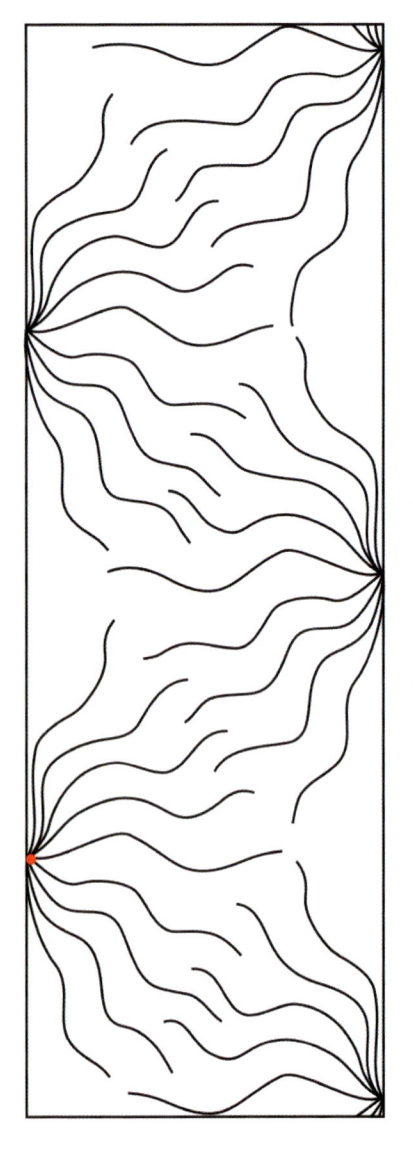

To quilt Water Plants, stitch a single wiggly line into the center of your quilting space.

Travel along this curving line back to the starting point, making sure to stay right on the line. Branch out with a new line, stopping so that it's not quite as long as the first.

You're aiming to create the same half circle shape you created with Shell Fan, only now with single wiggly lines.

Once you complete one Water Plant shape, travel along your quilting space and branch out with another until the first side is filled.

When you reach the opposite side, stitch a new Water Plant, fitting it in between two from the other side.

Play with this texture to see all the possible variations you can achieve when the lines curve together, cross, and interlock.

Cobwebs in the Corners

Let's see what happens when we add simple curving lines over the Water Plants design to create a new Cobwebs design:

To quilt this design, start by stitching Water Plants into the center of your quilting space.

Travel along the edge and stitch out to connect with the last curving line. Curve this line inward as you stitch to the end of the next line.

Connect all the ends of the Water Plant lines together, then travel inside and internally echo to fill the shape like a spider web.

Travel along the edge of your quilting space stitching more cobwebs. Take your time as this is a multi-step design and can be quite time consuming.

Once one side is filled, travel to the opposite side and fill in more cobwebs, fitting them in between the first set.

If you have trouble fitting any of the last 4 designs together, try marking a simple series of half circles over your quilt, then fill to the marked line.

- PART 9 -
STEM CENTERED DESIGNS

Now let's experiment with a family of designs that are literally grown - from stems that is!

Stem Centered Designs start with the center stem first, then the "leaves" are added by traveling and branching out along the stem. Try tracing the drawing above starting with the center stem, then branching out to create the feather leaves on one side and fern leaves on the other.

Texture - The designs in this chapter all have a beautiful flowing texture that builds off the central stem. The stem will always stand out with these designs due to the travel stitching and thread play that builds up in this area.

Suggestions for Use - Stem Centered Designs have a lot in common with **Foundational Designs** (pg. 36) because the texture of the design is determined by your starting stem.

These designs are going to work great in the open areas of your quilt where you have more than enough room for the stem and leaves to expand and fill the quilting space.

These designs can easily be used as **Motifs** (pg. 94) that stand out on the surface of your quilt and have other designs stitched around them for emphasis. You can even fill inside the stem with designs like **Chain of Pearls** (pg. 68).

LINE FERN

Let's get started stitching Stem Centered Designs with this simple Line Fern design which will fill your quilt with beautiful flowing texture and subtle movement.

To quilt Line Fern, start with a long flowing line. This is the base of your stem, so take this line throughout the space you wish to fill on your quilt.

Stop when you reach the point where you want your line to end, then echo this line all the way back, leaving at least ½" between the lines of quilting.

Now stitch inside this stem with two internal echoes, creating two lines of quilting within the stem.

Travel along the outside edge of the stem and branch off with a leaf shape. Travel inside this shape and fill it with an internal echo to create the extra lines of quilting within.

Travel along the edge of the stem, branching out with leaves along one side. When you finish with one side, travel to the opposite side and fill it with wiggly leaf shapes as well.

Tongue of Flames

Now let's experiment with shorter stems that swirl tightly around in short segments to create more interesting textures:

To quilt this design, start with a short stem, swirling into a slight spiral. Echo this stem back to your starting point, then travel along one edge, branching out with organic flame shapes.

Once you've filled both sides of the stem with flames, pick a gap between two flames and stitch through it with a new swirling stem line. Travel along this stem, branching out with more flames, interlocking with the first set so the flames entirely fill your quilting space with tight, swirling texture.

Swirling Feathers

If short stems work great for stitching flames, it should work well for feathers too! Use this design to swirl feathers throughout your quilt as an all-over quilting design.

To quilt this design, start with a short stem, swirling into a slight spiral. Echo this stem back to your starting point, then travel along one edge and branch out with small feathers.

Once you've filled both sides of the stem with feathers, pick a gap between two and stitch through it with a new short, swirling stem. Travel along stem, branching out with more feathers that stretch and interlock with the first to fill your quilting space.

Echo Feathers

Feathers are amazing designs! Use Echo Feathers to create beautiful **Motifs** (pg. 94) on the surface of your quilts.

To quilt Echo Feathers, start with a long flowing line. Come to a point, then echo this line back to your starting point to create a single stem.

Now travel along one side and branch out with soft, medium sized feathers.

Don't try to fill your quilting space entirely with the feather shapes. You want to leave space so you can echo the feathers and really make them stand out.

Once the stem has been entirely filled with feathers, echo the entire shape, bringing your quilting line down in between each feather so the thread builds up and each shape stands out beautifully.

Aim to surround your feather shape with at least five rows of echo quilting so it will stand out boldly against the tighter, echoing texture.

Butterfly Feathers

Variations of feathers are endless! Here's what happens when you quilt a circle into the tip of each feather:

To quilt Butterfly Feathers, start with a long flowing line, then echo this line to create a stem running throughout your quilting space.

Travel along this stem, branching out with a soft feather shape, then swirl into a circle at the end.

Focus on stitching the circles perfectly within each feather. When you focus on forming the circle, it's often easier to create a perfectly plump, gently curved feather shape.

Stack the feathers together and play with combining Butterfly Feathers and Echo Feathers to create an eye catching motif on the surface of your quilts.

If you find yourself struggling to create beautiful feathers, try rotating the quilt to get better visibility or a more natural angle to quilt in. It's amazing how even this small change can help with forming feathers!

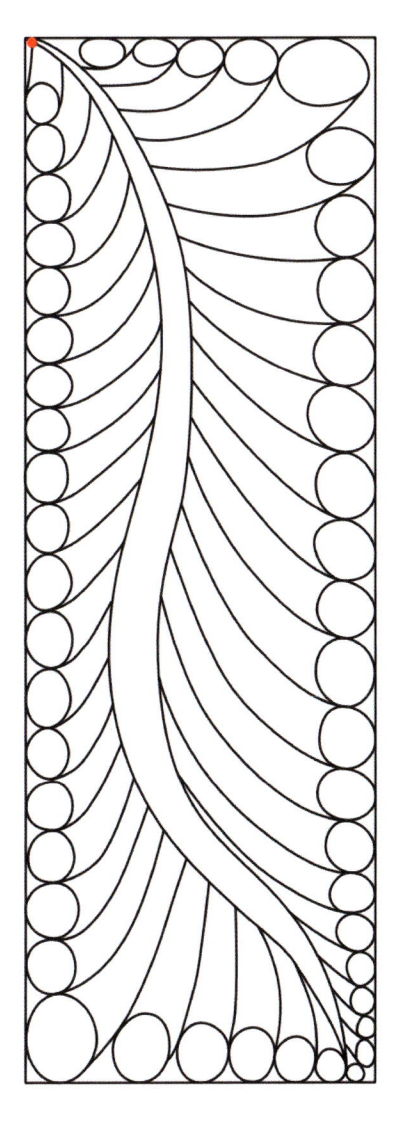

Heart Vine

Here's another Stem Centered Design using a heart shaped leaf that should be very easy for you to quilt. After all, how many times in your life have you drawn a simple heart shape?

To quilt Heart Vine, start with a long flowing line. Come to a point, then echo back to your starting point, creating a stem for your design.

Travel along this stem and branch out with a short stem, then flow into a heart shape.

Play with making the hearts both skinny and wide to see how this change can affect your entire design.

Travel and stitch heart shaped leaves throughout one side of the stem, elongating the leaves to completely fill one side of your quilting space.

Once one side is complete, travel stitch to the opposite side and fill it the same way with long flowing heart shapes.

Experiment with adding extra texture such as internal echoes to make the hearts stand out even better on your quilts.

- Part 10 -
Center Fill Designs

Now let's try a totally different way to create filler designs! What happens when you intentionally start quilting in the center of your quilting space?

Center Filled Designs always start in the center of your quilt, then radiate out with lines of quilting or "petals" to reach the edges of your quilting space.

Practice tracing this design starting in the center circle, then branch out with the simple petal shapes.

Texture - Center Fill Designs have the most dynamic, eye catching texture of all the designs in this book. Because these designs start in the center and usually involve a lot of thread play, they will always draw your eye like a bulls-eye.

You can easily turn these designs into **motifs** (pg. 94) that stand out boldly on the surface of your quilt with other, smaller scale designs like **Heart Paisley** (pg. 20) or **Echo Arches** (pg. 31) stitched around them so they show off even more.

Suggestions for Use - Because you have to start in the center to create a Center Filled Design, these designs work best in the open areas of your quilt. Open blocks, cornerstones, and circular or flower shaped appliqués are all great places for the designs in this chapter.

Sunflower

This first Center Fill Design is super easy to quilt and a great example of what you can do with simple tear drop shapes:

First stitch a small circle, then surround it with a set of small petals. Don't worry about stitching the petals perfectly as they will be covered up by the next set.

Once the first set of petals is complete, continue to stitch more petals, but make them longer, stretching further out into your quilting space. Continue to surround the central circle with more petal shapes, gradually getting longer and bigger until your entire quilting space is filled.

Spider Web

Working from the center, you can stitch many interesting shapes. Curving lines come together to create this cool Spider Web!

To quilt Spider Web, start in the center and stitch out with a long, flowing line. Travel stitch along the edge of your quilting space and stitch into the center with another long flowing line.

Continue to stitch flowing lines from the center to the edges until the space is loosely filled, finishing up back in the center. Next, stitch a simple curving spiral that gradually gets wider with each ring. Try to curve the line so it dips in slightly, almost like you're quilting "U" shapes between each flowing line to give the appearance of a real Spider Web.

Paisley Flower

Here's a design created by combining two awesome designs together: **Pebbling** (pg. 44) and **Paisley** (pg. 19). Just think about how many more designs you can create by combining previous designs together!

Starting in the center of your quilting space, stitch a cluster of Pebbling. Play with making the cluster very large and very small to see how this affects the texture of your design.

Next, branch out with a tear drop shape, pivot and echo to form a Paisley petal. Echo as many times as you like to expand this petal and take up space. Travel along the center and branch out with more Paisley petals to form a flower shape.

Feather Flower

Can feathers become the petals of a beautiful flower? Absolutely! Here's a perfect example of a Feathered Flower:

Start by stitching a cluster of pebbles or an alternative center design in the center of your quilting space. Branch off with a single flowing line, come to a point, then echo this line back to the center to create a skinny stem line.

Stitch plump, curving feathers along both sides of this stem, then travel stitch around the center and branch off with another stem line and more flowing feather shapes. Aim to surround the center with at least five feather "petals" to create a balanced, beautiful Feather Flower design.

Center Fill
- Learning Curve -

Take a look at all the Center Filled Designs we've learned so far. Each has had a slightly different center shape and base for the petals. How you start your flowers is very important for the overall texture and effect of the design.

The beauty of Center Filled Designs is that the centers are entirely interchangeable. If you like the center of one flower, but the petals of another try switching them out to see what happens. You'll probably come up with an entirely new design!

Single Circle - This is the simplest flower center, but it also adds the least amount of texture or interest to your quilt. Use this center when you want the focus of the design to be on the petals alone.

Cluster of Pebbles - **Pebbling** (pg. 44) creates a beautiful cluster of circles in the center of your flowers, which darkens this area making it stand out against the petal shapes.

Four Hearts - A simple cluster of four hearts creates a formal center to your flower shape. To stitch the hearts evenly, try marking a + shape on the center of your quilt, then line up each heart along the marked lines.

Spiral - A center spiral is a funky, fun way to begin any flower shape! First stitch a 1" circle, then swirl inside with a spiral into the center. If you'd like the spiral to show off boldly in the center, travel stitch along your spiral line to get back out of the circle.

Feathered Hearts

Feather Flower is such a beautiful design, let's try an easy variation, this time starting with hearts:

Start by stitching four hearts evenly spaced in the center of your quilt. Travel to the space between two hearts and stitch a feather up and around one shape. Continue to build feathers around that one side of one heart shape until you reach the edge of your quilting space.

Stitch feathers on the opposite side of the heart, balancing it with the first side. Travel stitch in between the rest of the hearts and build up more feathers until the entire quilting space is filled.

Flame Flower

Fiery flames make beautiful flower petals! Let's learn how to quilt this flower with a beautiful spiral center:

Start with a 1" circle in the center of your quilting space. Stitch a spiral into the center of this circle, then travel stitch back out so it stands out beautifully.

Next, branch out with 4-5 wiggly flame shapes around the center circle. Stitch inside each flame with an internal echo until the flame shape is entirely filled. Travel stitch to the outer edge of the flame petals and stitch more flames between the first set, filling each with internal echoes.

Brittle Starfish

What happens when you combine a spiral and **Chain of Pearls** (pg. 68) together? You'll get a beautiful Brittle Starfish!

Start with a 1" circle in the center of your quilting space. Stitch a spiral into the center of this circle, then branch out with a long gently curving line to the edge of your quilting space.

Come to a point, then stitch back to the center to form a wiggly tentacle like shape. Travel stitch inside this shape and fill it with a single row of circles. Branch off with 5-7 more wiggly lines and fill each with circles, then travel stitch to the outside and echo the flower until the entire background space is filled.

Motifs vs. Fillers

What is the major difference between a quilting motif and a filler design?

A filler design literally fills your quilt with texture. For the most part these designs are not marked on the surface of your quilts, but fill the space organically.

You know how to fill the areas of your quilts by memorizing the simple rules for each design, then fitting the shapes and lines into each area of your quilt.

A motif is a specific design that creates a focal point on the surface of your quilt. These designs are usually stitched on a larger scale so they stand out better.

To ensure the motif is perfectly symmetrical with the piecing or appliqué design, many quilter's mark the design on the surface of their quilts.

Most quilting stencils are actually motifs. You can mark the design easily on the surface of your quilt, then quilt it by following the marked line. If you find free form fillers very difficult to quilt, try quilting marked stencil designs instead. Being able to follow a line in free motion is just as important as being able stitch a free form design completely from memory.

Motifs stand out even better by being surrounded with filler designs. The smaller scale filler flattens the background area, making the larger scale motif stand out better:

Some filler designs can also be motifs! Here's what **Tongue of Flames**, pg. 80, and **Echo Feathers**, pg. 82, look like as motifs surrounded with **Double Pebble**, pg. 45, **Heart Paisley**, pg. 20, and **Feather Fans**, pg. 23:

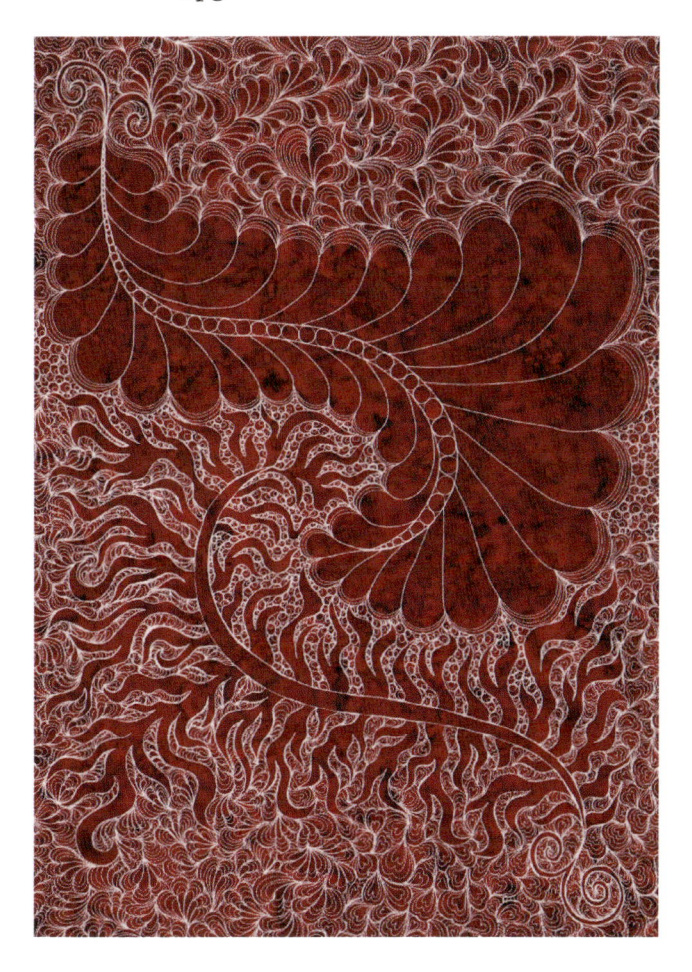

Take some time looking at the surface of your quilt to see where you could use larger scale motifs and smaller scale filler designs to create a gorgeous combination of textures on your quilts.

Intermediate Free Motion Quilting Fillers DVD

Feeling a little confused about how to quilt some of the designs in this book? Are you looking for a little more guidance on how to use these fillers in your quilts?

If so, this is definitely the DVD for you! Intermediate Free Motion Quilting Fillers showcases 33 designs from this book, stitched out clearly on this beautiful black and red quilt:

Follow along with Leah and learn how to quilt the following eight beautiful designs into open blocks:

Echo Arches
Sunflower
Heart Paisley
Poseidon's Eye
Feathered Hearts
Lightning Bolt
Brittle Starfish
Bleeding Hearts
Flaming Cocoon
Flame Spiral
Swirling Petals
Feather Flower
Paisley Flower
Tree Roots
Spider Web
Chain of Pearls

But what about your quilt's sashing? Learn how to fill this narrow area with the following amazing textures:

Water Plants
Flowing Glass
Double Pebble
Woven Lines
Circuit Board
Echo Feathers
Echo Rainbow
Tongue of Flames
Swirling Feathers
Pebbles in a Stream
Echo Maze
Gentle Flames
Seashells & Waves
Echo Crosses
Tree Bark
Sharp Stippling
Swirling Water

Learn more about this DVD at:

www.DayStyleDesigns.com

Index and Resources

McTavishing - pg. 50. This design was created by Karen McTavish. For more information about this design, please check out **Mastering the Art of McTavishing** published by On-Word Bound Books.

Bleeding Hearts - 24, *25*
Brittle Starfish - *93*
Butterfly Wings - *21*
Circuit Board - *15*, 32, 38
Double Pebble - *45*
Echo Crosses - *33*
Echo Maze - *32*
Echo Shell - *30*
Feather Fans - *23*, 26
Feather Universe - *42*
Feathered Hearts - *91*
Flame Flower - *92*
Flaming Cocoon - *48*
Flowing Glass - *70*
Goldilocks - *64*
Heart Paisley - *20*, 24, 85
Hearts & Spirals - 12, *16*
Landscape Stitch - *65*
Line Fern - *79*
Paisley - 7, 18, *19*, 25, 39, 57, 88
Pebble Loop - *28*
Pebbles in a Stream - *63*
Polka Dot Parade - *46*
Poseidon's Eye - *54*
Sharp Stippling - *14*, 95
Spider Web - *87*
Stippling - 7, 10, 12, *13*, 14, 57, 64
Super Circuit Board - *38*
Swirling Petals - *26*
Tongue of Flames - *80*
Trailing Tears - *71*
Tree Roots - 12, *17*
Wiggly Woven Lines - *61*

Blowing Wind - *56*
Butterfly Feathers - *83*
Chain of Pearls - 28, *68*, 78
Cobwebs in the Corners - *77*
Echo Arches - *31*, 85
Echo Feathers - *82*, 95
Echo Rainbow - *34*
Electric Storm - *73*
Feather Filler - *66*
Feather Flower - *89*
Fiery Comet - 8, *47*
Flame Spiral - *41*
Flaming Paisley - *22*
Gentle Flames - *59*
Heart Flow - *55*
Heart Vine - *84*
Icicle Lights - *72*
Lightning Bolt - *52*
McTavishing - 49, *50*, 51, 97
Paisley Flower - *88*
Pebbled Paisley - *27*
Pebbling - 27, 28, *44*, 57, 63, 88, 89
Pom Pom Parade - *75*
Seashells & Waves - *39*
Shell Fan - *74*
Starry Sky - *40*
Sunflower - *86*
Swirling Feathers - *81*
Swirling Water - *53*
Topographic Map - *37*
Tree Bark - *62*
Water Plants - *76*
Woven Lines - *60*, 61

Made in the USA
Lexington, KY
10 May 2014